BECOMING A

Beautiful Articulate Person

THE GENESIS OF TRANSFORMATION

I0085525

AMBER BRANCH

Printed in the United States of America, 2020

Articulate Business Group LLC

For more information, email, info@articulatebusinessgroup.com
or visit www.amberrbranch.com

Edited by Articulate Business Group LLC
Photos: Tal Campbell Photography, PEImages
Interior Design: FormattedBooks.com
Book Cover Design: 100covers.com

ISBN: 978-0-578-66851-2

BECOMING A BEAUTIFUL ARTICULATE PERSON

REVIEWS

BECOMING A

Beautiful Articulate Person

THE GENESIS OF TRANSFORMATION

This book was composed without any page numbers. In order to get the intended purpose of the book, please read the book from beginning to end without skipping ahead. There will be a reward for the reader in the end.

DEDICATION

For my two lovelies, you are my reason for everything. I love you both with no boundaries and you return my love equally with no judgement.

To the wise man that inspired this title (you know who you are). You saw potential in me when I couldn't even see it in myself. You supported and encouraged me more than some family members. Our bond is so undeniably strong. I will forever appreciate the endless support and love you have shown me over the years.

Last but not least to anyone who has ever felt unbeautiful and unworthy, this book is for you. May my words be uplifting and remind you, you're your own beauty and that's articulately beautiful!

ACKNOWLEDGEMENTS

As always, I must acknowledge my Lord and Savior Jesus Christ. He is my strength. He has and continues to lead, guide and protect me. Thank you for blessing me with my talent to write and inspire people. I will forever give you praise and glory! AMEN

Thank you for saving me. (John 3:16)

AUTHOR'S NOTE

This is for those:

- who have experienced pain
- who have a story to tell or
- who've felt like they're going insane
- who need inspiration sometimes
- who need reminders they're beautiful/handsome
- who can think for themselves with their own mind

This book is **NOT** for you if:
- you've never felt sad or
- you've never been drowning in tears
- your life is perfect or
- your world has always been crystal clear
- you live to judge others
- or you've never felt your heartbreak
- you don't believe in loving one another or
- you look down on other's mistakes

This book **IS** for everyone!

This book is to remind us all that we have at some point in our lives gone through struggles and some form of pain. Our growth phases may be completely different.

That's where our beauty resides:

It is our struggles that make us strong.
It is our struggles that make us human
It is our struggles that sing the most beautiful songs
Our struggles tell our stories and unite us all as
BEAUTIFUL ARTICULATE PEOPLE (B.A.Ps)

"Beauty is only skin deep...
transform your soul
and everything
else will follow..."

—AMBER BRANCH

PROLOGUE

This is not meant for the faint at heart
it's not for self-righteous souls
whose sanctimonious views they try to embark
this is not for those who choose to remain in the dark

This is about my life
it has not been squeaky clean
even though that may be how it seems
my poems are a reflection of my triumphs and strife

As you continue forth engaging in my journey
do so with an open mind and compassionate spirit
even if you feel like you don't want to hear it,

REMEMBER: *"For all have sinned and fall short of the glory of God...
judge not so you won't be judged"*

PHASE I:
Transformation
Loading....

WHAT'S A B.A.P?

BEAUTIFUL ARTICULATE PERSON (B.A.P)

Historically a B.A.P has been defined as a Black American Princess. BAP has sometimes been used as a derogatory term for black women of upper and upper middle class background, who possess (or are perceived to possess) a spoiled or materialistic attitude. Hollywood capitalized off the stigma in the 1997 box office hit, B.A.P.S, starring Oscar Award Winning Actress, Halle Berry.

This book serves to redefine the term B.A.P as a Beautiful Articulate Person.

BECOMING A B.A.P

1. Be your own kind of beau·ti·ful
/ˈbyo͞odəfəl/ adjective

Pleasing the senses or mind aesthetically; of a very high standard; excellent.
2. Be ar·tic·u·late.
/ärˈtikyələt/adjective

Someone capable of speaking easily and clearly, and is most often referred to someone who is well-spoken.

A B.A.P (redefined) is any individual that has surpassed all definitions of what it means to be normal. They are open-minded with a keen discernment for all things not easily observed by the general public. They speak clearly and coherently with affection and compassion. They motivate others to become their own form of beauty.

Excerpt from an Icon—"Flaws and All"

by Beyonce Knowles-Carter

"I'm a train wreck in the morning
I'm a bitch in the afternoon
Every now and then without warning
I can be really mean towards you
I'm a puzzle, yes, indeed
Ever-complex in every way
And all the pieces aren't even in the box
And yet you see the picture clear as day
I don't know why you love me
And that's why I love you
You catch me when I fall
Accept me, flaws and all
And that's why I love you
And that's why I love you
And that's why I love you
I neglect you when I'm working
When I need attention, I tend to nag
I'm a host of imperfection
And you see past all that
I'm a peasant by some standards
But in your eyes I'm a queen
You see potential in all my flaws
And that's exactly what I mean
I don't know why you love me
And that's why I love you
You catch me when I fall

Accept me, flaws and all
And that's why I love you
And that's why I love you
And that's why I love you"

Welcome Back

*(In loving memory of Aaliyah Dana Haughton
January 16, 1979 – August 25, 2001)*

It's been a long time
I shouldn't have left you
with a dope rhyme to snap to..
…snap to…snap to…
…snap to…snap to…

Long & overdue
I present to you
not brand new
just remixed Rhymes from a Sapphire
that was once so blue
proud of the woman I see
& continuing to rep' the A to the B…
my mask is off
living unapologetically free
No more sad love songs
No more soggy tears
only inner peace
from past wrongs…

It took me a minute
life knocked me down
I'm stronger now—
mind, body and spirit

All the trials & heartaches,
frustration and pain
God took me through,
'til His plan was clearly explained

He's not through
and I'm still learning
but I've grown up
& stopped feeling so gloomy & blue;

I'm clearly focused
my vision is now 2020
this is my lyrical story
with no hocus pocus!!

PHASE II: B.A.P Process Initiation

The Next Chapter

I am woke
I am happy
a necessary change
converting my swag to savvy and classy

I am anxious and excited;
wanting so much more
life has been bittersweet
I am ready
for what's behind the next door

Moving on has been tough
but I do this for my kids
that I love Oh, so much

Transforming back to my "Shades of Amber"glow
shining beautiful and bright
I'm going to show the world how I grow!

Being in Love & Loving Without

Once upon a time
I was in love with a wonderful man
but with him I could never be
because I was hitched to a man
I at times could not stand

The ultimate catch 22
on one hand winning love
on the other hand felt like losing too;

So what do you do?
When faced with a difficult experience
& the solution should be obvious
but it's complicated
& makes no sense

I didn't know if the one I loved had a clue
and then there was hubby;
did I mention we have a child
—not just 1 but 2...

...My dilemma:
never want to hurt my kids;
& and the parentals love Mister,
the other problema
The plot now thickens
divorce not an option
—for the Pastor's daughter

the "good ol'" churchy folks
would've thought I was trippin'

What would Jesus do (WWJD)?
Hmmm….

To be honest
I don't even have a foggy clue
I was in love with someone
I had to live without
trying to be faithful
but my heart was dehydrated
in a lovesick drought

Forever Yearning

I couldn't get him off my mind
he is constantly steaming in my thoughts
O why do I always fall for that kind?

Wishing I could forget about him
the way he looked
the way he made me feel
he was engrained in me
a part of me like one of my limbs

I was longing to be with him all the time
in the morning
when I would rise
he would even come to me
in my dreams—
which were heavenly divine?

I was too scared to ask
if he felt the same
or if my feelings
were completely insane…

…I told myself I would never love again
or at least not until
my next life began

He did something to me
I wasn't ready for
I never imagined
those feelings would come to be

a compromising stance
yearning once again
contemplating if it was a forever
or just a momentary sin
longing for the day
when my yearning would end.

True Love at Last

I had a dream one night
an unbelievable story
the one I'd been yearning for
was in plain sight

It was surreal
I could reach him
His face I could touch
& his kiss I could feel

Happily ever after
appeared to be finally true
I looked in his eyes
& I immediately knew—
—I knew he was the One
and fit for me
like the perfect glove

The prayer of my
every waking moment;
my words were heard
Prince Charming was heaven sent

Then in an unexpected sequence,
I woke
My smile unfairly vanished
& reversed into a frown
It felt like a cruel prank—
was this a joke?

Immediately,
I felt myself yearning
for the man in my dreams
I needed that love
I had just seen

Swarmed with sadness and wondering…
Is it ever really possible—real love?
If so, where can I find it?
Does it exist in this world
or only in a place far away and above?

I need that type of love
I gotta have it in my life
Then, it hit me like POW!
That type of love
can only come from Christ?

He died on the cross for my sins
WOW!
He did all that for me?

Who else would do something like that
just to set me free!

THAT'S MY TRUE LOVE!

"My true love
At first sight
Is none other than
Christ..."

—AMBER BRANCH

PHASE III:
Metamorphosis
Mentality
The Awakening

Anxiety

Mental illness is real
Depression is a disease
Pains from the past reopen like an ulcer
each time they become
harder and harder to heal

It feels like everything is paused around me
except the thoughts in my head
the constant thoughts
create lazy moments
to stay and lay in my bed…

…I can't sleep
at least not a good R.E.M round
—> my eyes are wide open
—> my mouth won't make a sound not a whisper
& not even a peep

1st thought:
Maybe I should die
—> I could never do that to my kids
(I cry)
I cry so much that I'm drenched wet
and up to my eyeballs in drowning tears

2nd thought:
Why?
—> Why am I here?
(I sigh)

3rd thought:
(more like a prayer)

"Lord, I can't go on this time."

This prayer I've prayed
many times before;
this time was different;

In the midst of my sobs
and wailing cries,
I heard a soft, gentle whisper;

…the children sound asleep
husband was nowhere to be found
So, who could it be?
There was no one around

it was just me alone
with the sounds in my mind….
….then, I heard it again, "Amber…"

It was a deep bass voice
unlike any man I'd ever heard

The echo of my name
in the darkness
and the calming
bass tone comforted me
no other words were needed to follow
it was creepy and content
in the silent rooms hollow

No figure appeared
for the BIG REVEAL
The sound of my name
in the silence of the night
commanded my thoughts
to stand still

The sound of that voice
drummed back through my ears
it put me at peace.
all my fears & pain
were instantaneously released.

Depression is

real...

but there is a cure

His name is Jesus...

He's a healer...

My Struggle is Real

Sometimes it seems
so hard to do right
I try
and I try—
—try with
all my might

I seem to repeat
the same process
whether J., Ramon,
James or Rashad
they're all the same,
all hurting me just like the rest

My struggle is my obsession
with a good hard cock
it's an unproductive
habit I can't seem to stop

I told myself
I would never
ever do this again
but here I lay
in another bed
made for sin

Temptation won
Me,
Away again I want to run

My Main Squeeze

I come to you
in the middle of the night
when my world's been turned upside down
and nothing feels right;

In those dark, quiet hours
everything is STILL
except my thoughts,
alarming me like
"SAVE THE CLOCK TOWER"

You calm my thoughts
you stroke my soul
your soothing touch
comforts me
and once again I feel whole;

When I'm stressed
you hold my hand
you give me strength
that's why I don't mind
calling you my man

So many others before
have hurt &
betrayed me
you've actually taught me a few things;
things I overlooked or didn't care to see

You guide me in the right way;
& you help me articulate
what I'm trying to say

You're the reason I continue growing
You give me the truth
(information based on facts);
things worth knowing;

Always and forever, you're my one true bae
you're my "write or die"
every single day

Thank you for never judging my sins
My dearly beloved
Sweet Pen!

Therapeutic Friendships

My hittas
are like original gangstas
& always by my side
They are my "ride or die"
natural go-gettas

Every day we meet
at the same café
we share it all
everything we have to say

I can depend on them,
they're my BFF bros
they don't judge me or
tell my secrets

they hold my words deep within
so no knows…

I can't trust many broads
chicks smile in your face
then talk about you
behind your back like evil frauds

I'll stick to my network team of
he, he and me
we go hard for each other
like a threesome menagerie

I'm living my life like it's golden
with a wonderful
new crew
suppressing our
thoughts in black and blue

Allow me to introduce
two men they are so bad
My Pen and My Pad

Intermission:
The Crossroads

Intermission:
A Self-Searching
Soliloquy

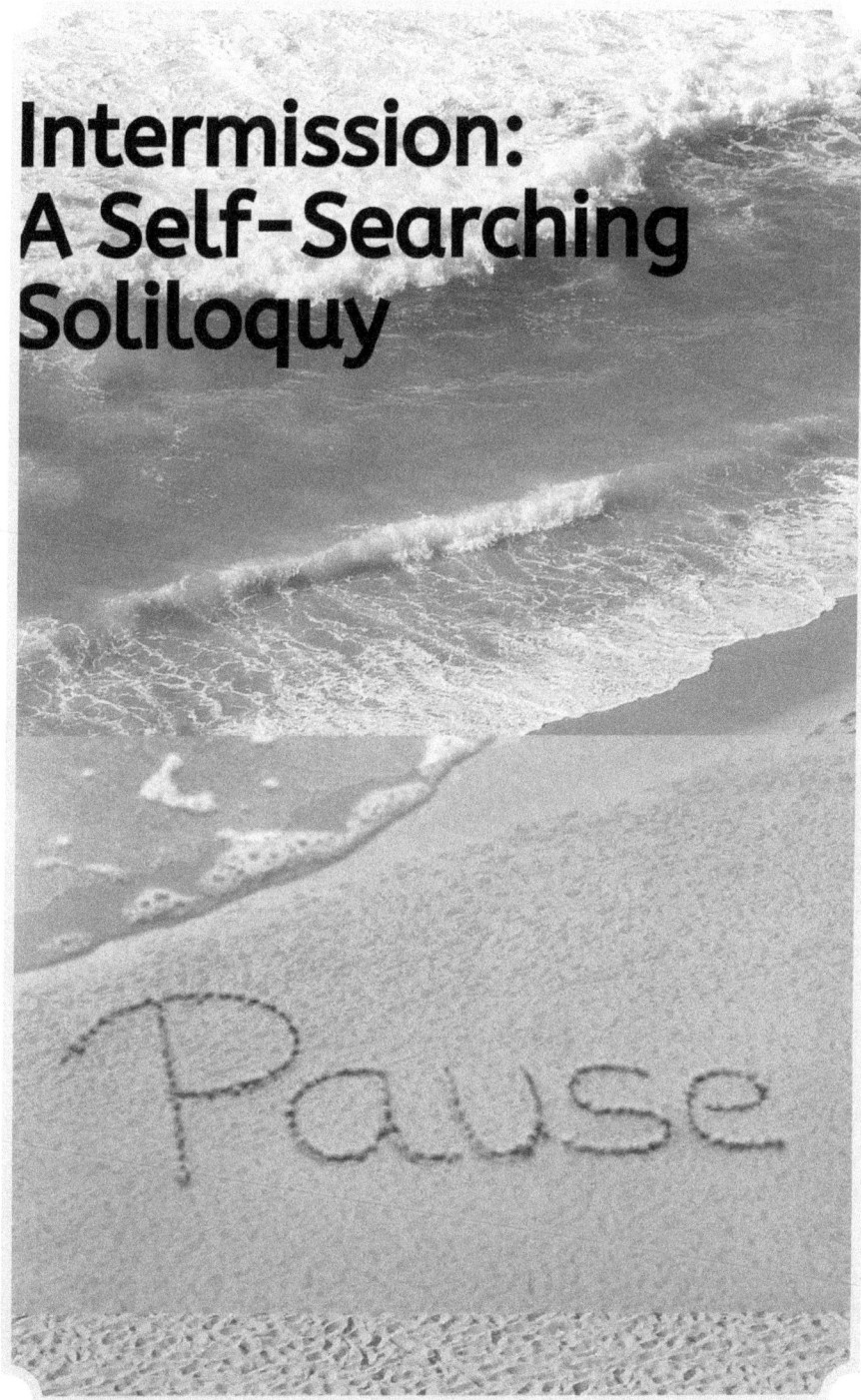

Pause

A's Ok

"Are you okay?"
these 3 meaningless words
are spoken to me
day after day after day
they are pointless
and nauseating

What do these words mean?
What are the people
that utter them really asking?

Do they really care—
if "I'm O'KAY?

Are they concerned genuinely?
or just being nosy
hoping for juicy gossip
to regurgitate like spilled tea

Did they hear about my illness
the one that has plagued
my family for generations
the illness that makes me
shoot needles into my skin

Are they asking if,
"I'm O'kay" because
they think I'm a crackhead?

Or Did they hear about my sins
Do they want to judge me
for all the secrets I hold within

They just keep asking,
"Are you O'Kay?"

What if I yell "NO I'M NOT OKAY!"
what's the next thing
they'll have to say?

I bet they won't offer to help
they probably won't
even lend a hand
all they'll think to say is,

"I UN-der-STAND"
Do they really UN-der-STAND?
Or is that a premeditated response
so they can carry on with their life
that they think is SO grand?

Do they UN-der-STAND
what it feels like to lie in the
hospital day after
day after day
not knowing if
you will live or die
lose your limbs
or the eyesight in your eye?

This is a message to
hypocritical simpletons &
superficial imitation saints;
to holy-rolley church folk type those
who bypass the
"Are you Okay?" &
just say,
"For you I'll pray"

I often wonder
what are they praying for?
for my redemption or my demise;
they smile and pretend to care
meanwhile side-eyeing me
with an evil glare

Maybe folks intentions are good
when they ask
"Are you O-kay?"

Maybe my feelings have
gone so far astray that I
can't even believe the
words people say

Yet I still feel like
I'm a joke to most
my pain is on display
for the world to see
a sweet delight for some,
like cinnamon and toast

I've realized that it is my pleasure
to experience my pain
to endure the highs and lows
of this type 1 disease
It is my duty to show the world

I AM OKAY

I AM STRONG

I AM A FIGHTER

I WILL CONTINUE TO FIGHT

&

I WILL WIN

I will win
day
after day after day
time
and time again!

WHY?

Scared for my life
as i laid in the hospital
about to once again
go under the knife

I wondered, "Why am I here?"
Why is this the same place I keep seeing?
Why does fighting to live always feel like
the theme of my being?

What does my future hold?
Is this where I'm destined to dwell?
I prayed and I asked God to keep my soul
to protect it from diving into the pits of hell

(that's the Cliff's Notes version of my conversations with God)

The spirits of my past,
my present
and my future hung out
by my hospital bedside

They replayed my life
like an old black and white movie
full of happy times
misery
sadness
& strife

I was thumbing through
my chapters like a T.V guide
when Mr. Reaper came in
and took me for a ride

We went up and down
in and out
back and forth
through a kaleidoscopic maze
I was searching for answers to
my questions—

My questions of WHY?
& my question of HOW?

How did my life spiral
so far down
& so out of control?
Why is pain
my life's payment?
Why is my journey
on a road with
an expensive ass toll?

I know I've made mistakes
& at times gone astray
Why am I punished
when everyone else's life is
like a piece of cake?

Why am I punished so hard?
there are people
who continuously sin
and show little
to no regard

Why do they remain
healthy and carefree

O Why?
O Why?
WHY ME?

Don't get me wrong,
I'm grateful
I appreciate all my blessings
I praise and thank God
from the time I wake up
until the evening
when I lie down
I'm grateful for my children
They mean the world to me
I want to make sure
I'm making the right
decisions for them

Society sold me this fairy tale concept long ago
it's about the perfect family
a husband, a wife,
2.5 kids
& a dog living harmoniously
under one quaint little cottage roof
with a white picket fence...
and they all live happily ever after.

So I grew up,
got married
and headed down that ideal path
made some babies
nurtured plants (instead of a dog)

The fairy tale was too surreal
for me to grasp
it was too good to be true
& Life is far from a cereal
or a board game
& there is no such person
as Prince Charming

sometimes, I feel like men
are natural born scum,
they're all pretty much the same
more like Dr Jekyll than Mr. Hyde
and just plain dumb

& now Mr. and Mrs. have kids to support
bills to pay
& a fairy tale lie to sustain

But why do people stay married
for the sake of saving face
until they pass on
and get buried;
many families have done this
for centuries
it's senseless and insane

Me, myself,
I've gone along to get along
for so long
it's 2nd nature to me
I've depended on others
to assist my decision making

Sometimes it feels like
my life is a well-orchestrated plan

strategically mapped out from birth
inch by inch
moment by moment
right down to my marriage
I never trusted my own mind
Never believed in my own beauty
So I married the man
my family wanted for me
I fell for him
because he was the one
everyone loved
I trusted everyone else's judgment
but not my own.
I forgot to listen to my heart

So now I'm cruisin' with Grimm
lying in this bed awaiting
my fate of doom
as the lights begin to dim
there is no one to blame
but myself
for my tragic departure.
I want to start over
or at least try to live my life
for God, my kids & I
until the Lord's final rapture
We can live life free like mermaids
floating in the sea
I want to be with my true love

with someone who
WILL NOT deceive me or lie
I don't know if I want the person
everyone else thinks for me
he's the perfect guy;

I want someone who loves me
for me and
let's me live unapologetically free

WHY can't I have that?
HOW do I get that?
WHERE do I start?

Divorce?

No way—not for a preacher's kid
—that's preposterous & sacrilegious
to the self-righteous "let the church say Amen" crowd
—> But what if a man was a self-centered,
opportunist and only entered
into a union for a come up?

Is that what God designed marriage for?
—> What if a man didn't show interest
unless he had an audience
to witness his side-show circus performance?

No love,
No intimacy
A marriage with no passion, love or intimacy
is nothing more than a business arrangement
It's a mere transaction
of mortal souls for selfish gain

I'm confused...
What would you do?

WWJDo?

I don't know what I'd do

Seek God's guidance
& do things according to His will;
Pray to God that the heart He'll heal

I know what I can no longer do
I can't continue bad habits again
I can't continue living to please others
I will press restart
so my new life can begin

Phase IV:
Lessons
Learned

0%   Loading..... 100%

The Learning Stage

This phase of my B.A.P process
it's not designed
to be lyrical
or entertaining
This part of the journey is a
vibe of no nonsense

It is a quintessential piece
preparing for the crown
at the end
of my journey

Without this portion
my life would cease

If you made it this far
continue a little more
the information that follows
will complete my B.A.P process—
mind, body and soul!

NOTE:

The following pages are excerpts from my diary.
My journal is full of scriptural references combined with my thoughts.

The scriptures helped shape me into a
Beautiful Articulate Person inside and out.

In the words of dear ol' Pastor dad:
May the words that follow
"bless and keep you real, real good"

Pretty Powerful

It's a beautiful thing
It can make
a sad person happy
a mad person rejoice
and sing
help a person who does bad
turn from her naughty ways,
pray & journal
her story
in her writing pad;

It's the power of love
the best gift
you can give anyone just
as it was given to us
from above (John 3:16)

For God is love
He created us all in His image
so we must love one another
just as He loves us.

But first you must learn to love yourself
before you can even begin
to give love to someone else

"Distance won't break a true bond

Friendship

"*A friend is someone*
who knows all about you
and loves you
just the same."

Elbert Hubbard [1856-1915]

An American writer, publisher, artist, and philosopher. He was an important advocate of the Arts and Crafts movement of his time.

Eternal Besties (BFFs)

In grade school
my parents had a magnet
on our fridge
I thought it was so cool

it had a quote
from Elbert Hubbard about
friendship

I studied that magnet daily
2 cute cuddly kittens stared
back at me
captivated by the rhyme
I would recite that poem
in my mind
& at times out loud

I was enamored
& oddly proud
with the concept—true friends

at that moment on words
I learned to depend
they became my companions…

…As I grew older
and wiser
the poem stayed with me
like a friend's shoulder
the words comforted me
during my loneliest times
though I never understood why—
I didn't have many close friends,;
because I was shy
I often preferred solitude over

the camaraderie of my peers;
& would rather engage in the warmth
of my lonely tears

Now I realize
these lyrics made me feel something
The words gave me solace
A kind, gentle comfort
that can only come from
One It can only come from
His only begotten Son

"I am a friend of God"

Transformation Process

*"And do not be conformed
to this world,
but be transformed
by the renewing of your mind,
that you may prove
what is that good and acceptable
and perfect will of God."*

**Romans 12
King James Version (KJV)
Holy Bible**

"Love life.
Engage in it.
Give it all you've got.
Love it with a passion
because life truly does give back,
many times over,
what you put into it."

—Maya Angelou
April 4, 1928–May 28, 2014

LET NOTHING DIM THE LIGHT
THAT SHINES FROM WITHIN.

MAYA ANGELOU

Beauty

"Favour is deceitful,
and beauty is vain:
but a woman that
feareth the LORD,
she shall be praised."

Proverbs 31:30
New International Version (NIV) Holy Bible

"Your <u>own</u> beauty tells your story, our stories unite us all as articulate beauties..."

--Amber Branch

Transformation in progress

Update

0%   Loading.... 100%

Perfection

"For all have sinned,
and come short
of the glory of God;"

Romans 3:23
New International Version (NIV) Holy Bible

"*God cannot use you if you're perfect...let Him use your imperfections to inspire others...*"

-- Laureesa Ogans (1932-2001)

Don't Judge

Judge not, that you be not judged. For with what judgment you judge, you will be judged; and with the measure you use, it will be measured back to you. And why do you look at the speck in your brother's eye, but do not consider the plank in your own eye? Or how can you say to your brother, 'Let me remove the speck from your eye'; and look, a plank is in your own eye? Hypocrite! First remove the plank from your own eye, and then you will see clearly to remove the speck from your brother's eye."

Matthew 7:1-5
New International Version (NIV) Holy Bible

"Beauty
Is in the eye
of the beholder..."

"Women should be tough and tender, laugh as much as possible and live long lives."

—MAYA ANGELOU

A Classic

Beauty

is Articulately Beautiful

—AMBER BRANCH

"She speaks
with wisdom,
and faithful
instruction
is on her tongue…

She watches
over the affairs
of her
household

& does not
eat the bread

Idleness"

Proverbs 31:26-27
New International Version (NIV)
Holy Bible

PHASE V:
Evolution

Regaining Clarity

My Rebirth

One Sunday morning at the beach
my soul was renewed
and finally
became at peace

I watched the waves
flow in
while the sun
sat down on me
and grinned

The water
looked so free
like it was well-kept
freshly manicured
with white tips
she moved back and forth,
swaying her
blueish-brown hips

I felt the sand
kissing my toes
while the water continued
tempting and inviting me
to come in
and greet her bare
to comfort my woes

I gazed around
to see if anyone was near

I looked up
for a sign from the heavens
and noticed
the seagulls soaring
far and crystal clear

I grew envious of them
flying so freely
thinking to myself
they must never feel
trapped
or claustrophobic,
that's how I long to be ideally

They get to escape
into the world
I'll bet their lives
rarely ever get bored

My bond with nature
drew me closer to God that day
and even though
I missed church
nature's sermon
reassured me
that my life would be okay

As the waves
continued
to rolled in
and the tides rolled on
I knew at that very
moment,
my spirit had been
reborn

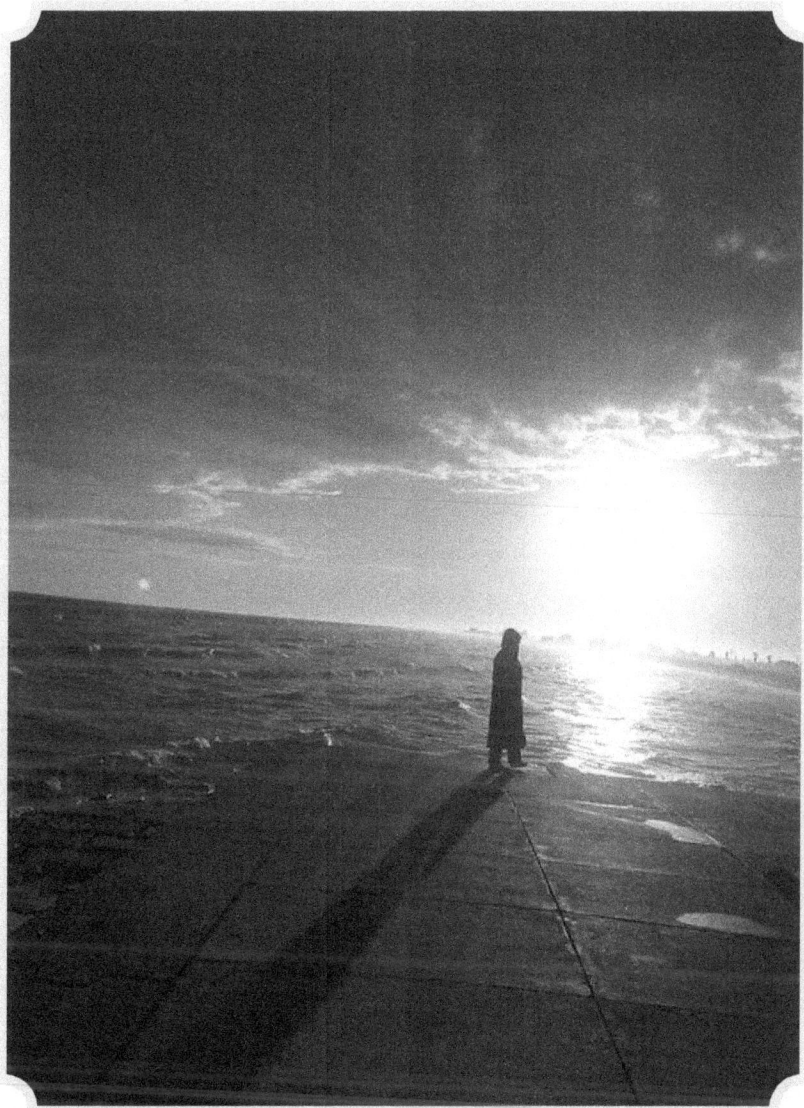

#Momlife

It's tough
an oxymoron
It's rewarding
at times it's rough

starting off so sweet
stealing your heart
at first glance
from the moment
you meet

As they grow
and develop
into their own
so grows the distance
between you
as they become
less like your clone

You swear you'd give your life
for that little seed even when
they are disrespectful
& will not
take heed

Constantly praying for them
you guide them every day
hoping that in their lives
success and prosperity
will come their way.

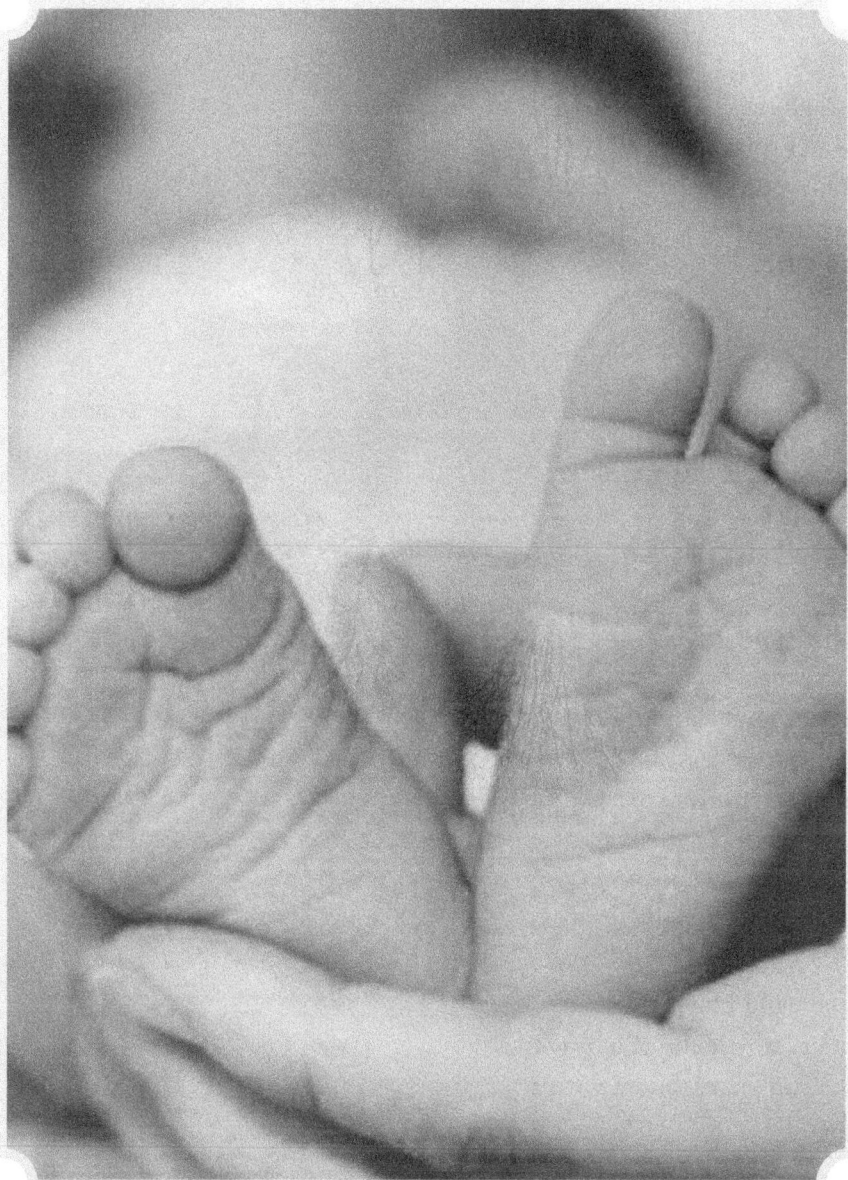

Aquatic Love

Laughing
Water splashing
Joking turns
to anger then
back to
laughter
then back to splashing

the sounds of the pool
are melodic songs heard
during summer
when kids are out of school
they are kind
& at times cruel

a paradox
pleasure & pain
wrapped neatly
in a bow, placed
nicely
in a child-size box

The wind blows
their curly locks of hair while
the sun guards them with a
friendly stare

the sounds
of the pool scene
the amusement
of my children being children
delights me
and makes my heart beam

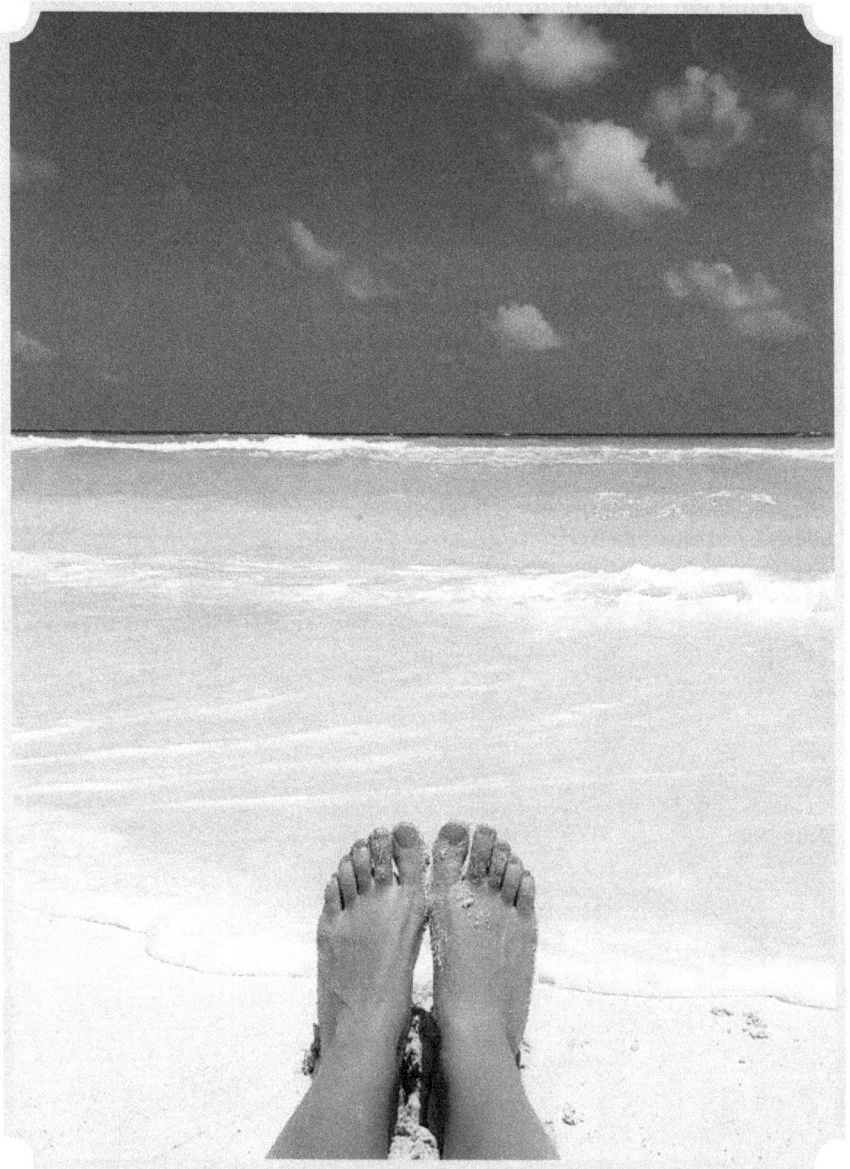

Recess

(just for fun)

Orange
Red
Blue or
Green

Extra dirty
or super clean
made for
children of
all ages
a rare,
exotic trend not
often found
in the yellow pages
It's not for oral pleasure

Keep your minds
out the gutter
this is pure innocence
for those
3 years old and plus

WARNING:
moms and dads BEWARE
small parts may cause your kids
to choke and fuss.

Message in a bottle

(To the ones who hurt me)

A special delivery
to the countless ones
I've foolishly trusted.
no names—applicable
to many;

Love it or hate it—
it is what it is
it is how it's been
you can share glance
at it or stare
hell, start a Facebook group
about it
I don't care

I've learned
a valuable lesson
from your betrayal
no longer do I live
in denial or confliction
seeking people's approval
I've been cured
from that addiction
they never listened
when I talked
and never cared
about my thoughts
Since the world around me went deaf

READ this:

> *"I'm reborn*
> *becoming a Beautiful Articulate Person,*
> *I AM the genesis THAT IS being transformed!"*

PHASE VI: TRANSFORM

Daily Dose

To be fit and fine
I have to work out daily
never forget my vitamin dose
& what I need the most
thin up top
& dripping ready to ooze
tap the sides
to make it stop

Anxious as I prep
to put it in
sounds like a crackhead
instead of a Type I diabetic (T1D)
with an insulin pen

exhale in a deep breathe
as I pinch my skin
& plunge the needle
to go deep in

I try to live my best T1D life
It's just not easy
life is a daily dose of pokes and
pricks that cut like a knife
1 minute I'm high
the next I'm low
the constant ups & downs
make me feel like a yo-yo

I look to my right when I'm done
it's my child's time
this part is no fun…

a mommy/
daughter T1D duo
DiaBesties forever
Type 1 till Type none
We'll keep fighting
for a cure
always and
together

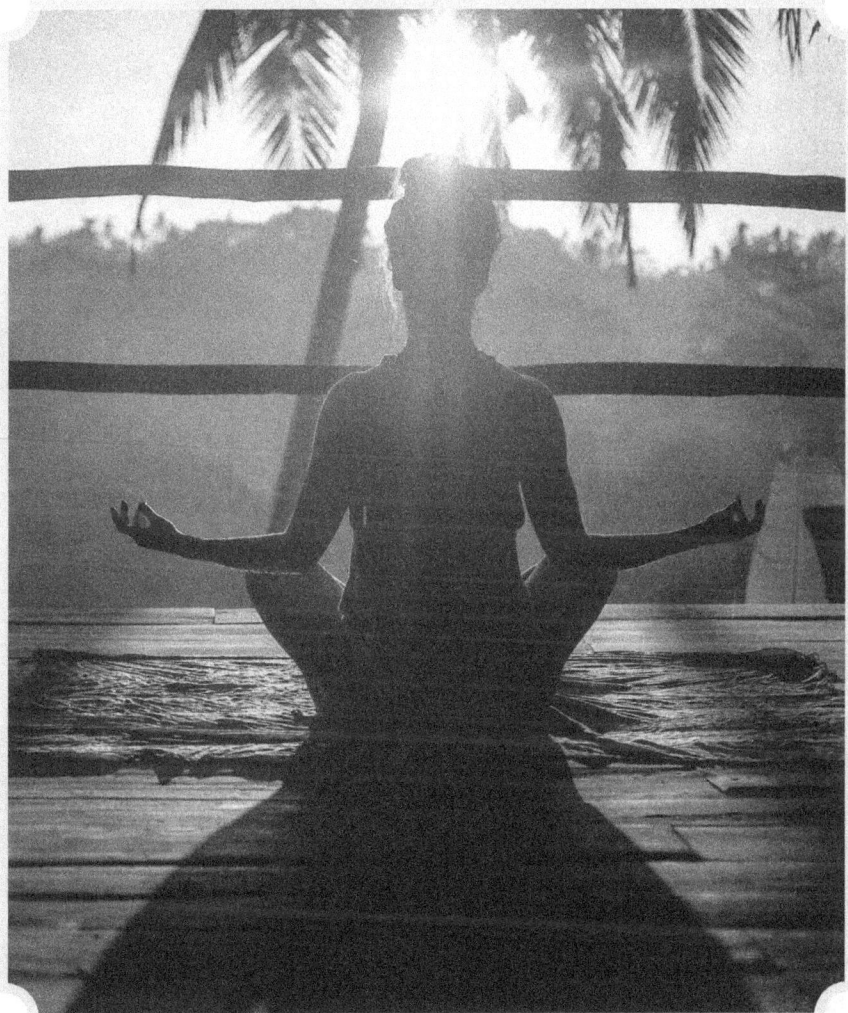

Pain vs. Pleasure

I've experienced so much pain
I've been broken
and bruised
and shackled in chains

I've learned
to embrace the bad
and appreciate the
good to always rejoice
and always be glad

I can now endure
and enjoy the pain
to get to the pleasure I
take them 50/50
so they meet
in the middle lane
Pain gives me joy
and creates
an adrenaline rush like
a teenage crush it
makes me act coy

My pain and pleasure,
they're now living together
in harmonious bliss
a once troublesome marriage of
Love and War
til' death do them part now
sealed with a kiss!

*"My weakness
is now
my weapon...
...and my pain is
my pleasure."*

—UNKNOWN

NEW
VERSION

PHASE VII:
BECOMING
ARTICULATE
BEAUTY
(A.B)

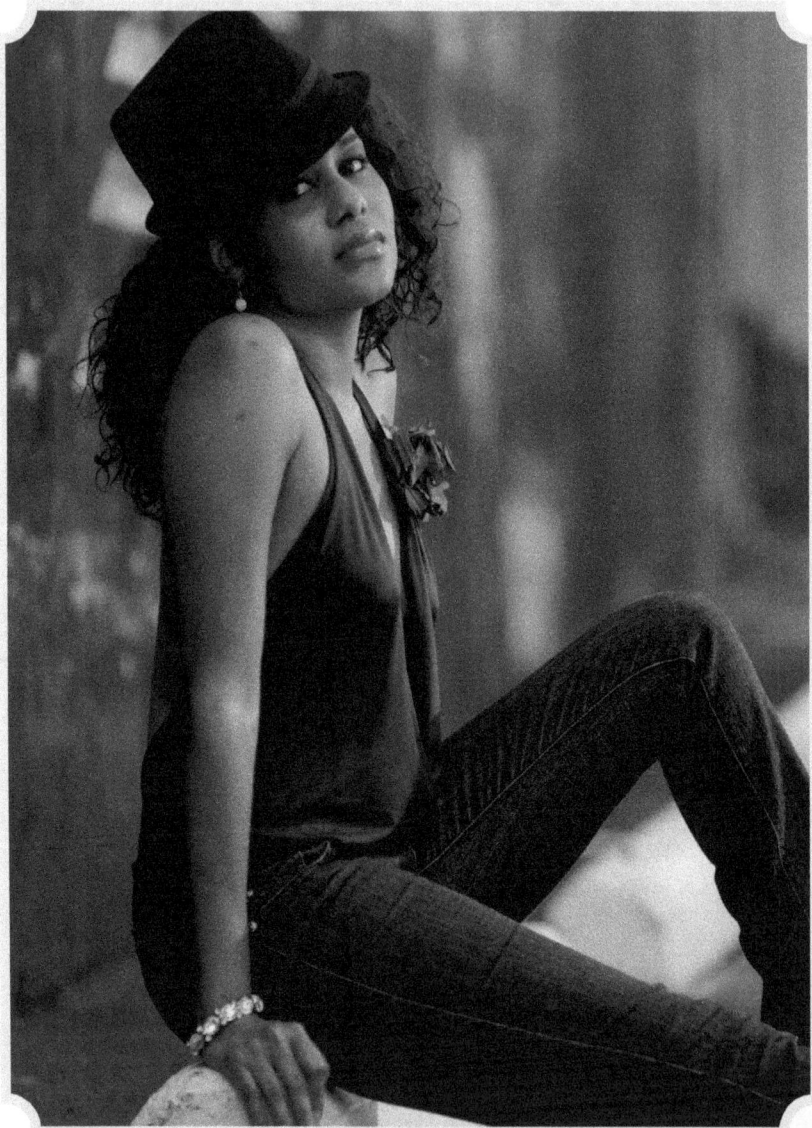

Transformation Complete

Life is precious
Life is poetic
Life is beauty

Beauty is precious
Beauty is poetic
Beauty is life

Listen to the poetry of life
See the beauty in life
Cherish the precious moments about life

Become precious
Become poetic
Become a beautiful being

PHASE VIII:
Become

a Beautiful Articulate Person
(B.A.P)

Awaken
Learn
Evolve
Transform
Become

Tell your story

HOW TO BECOME:

WRITE, TYPE & PRAY

The journey begins with

PRAYER

&

a journal

Pray, Seek, Find

"Ask
and it will be
given to you;
seek
and you will find;
knock
and the door will be opened to you."

Matthew 7:7
New International Version (NIV) Holy Bible

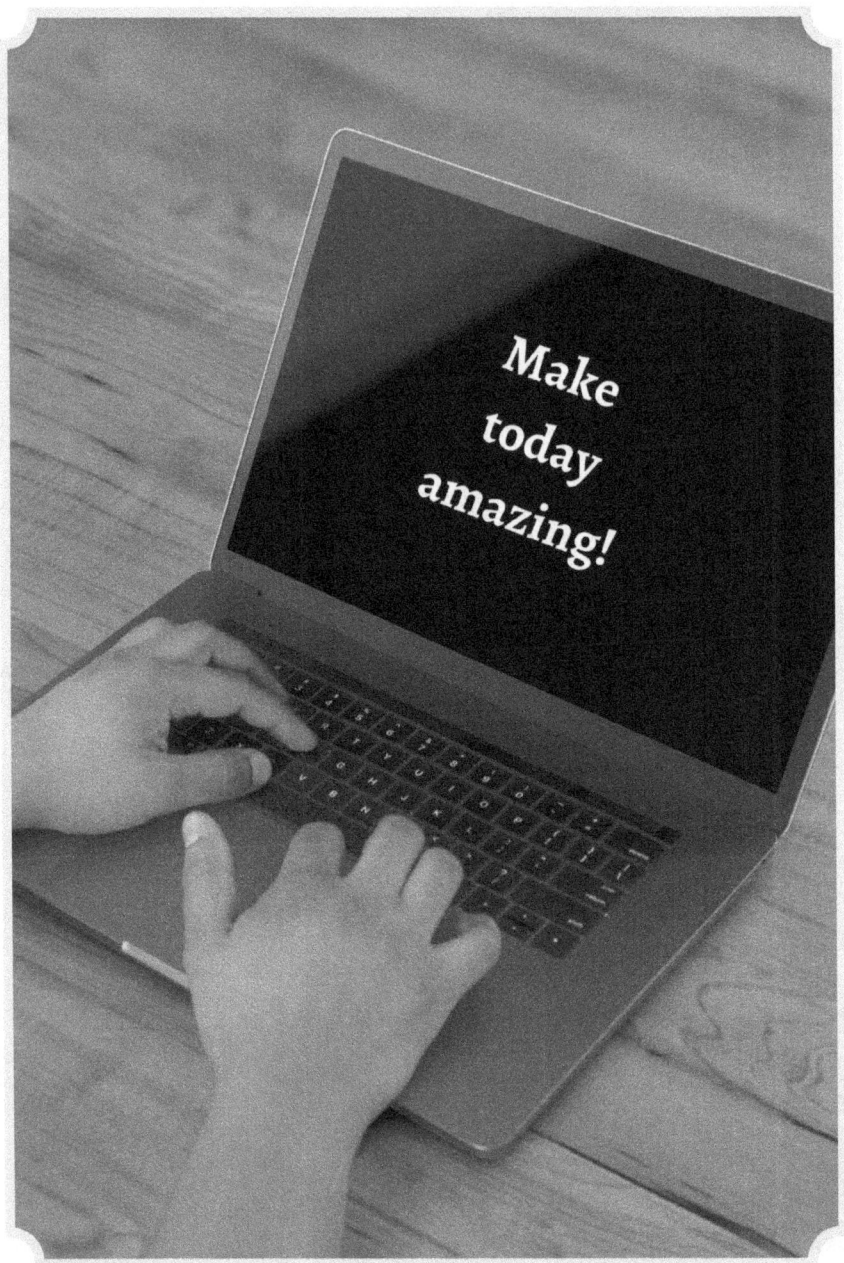

Be Strong-Yield to Temptation

"Be strong
and courageous.
Do not be afraid;
do not be discouraged,
for the LORD
your God will be with you
wherever you go."

Joshua 1:9
New International Version (NIV) Holy Bible

ABOUT THE AUTHOR

Amazon author and award-winning writer, Amber Branch is a Mom, wife, entrepreneur and brand ambassador. There is not much she won't do or try.

Her drive and determination is what pushes her through to success. She is a modern day renaissance woman. Her passion for writing formed at a very early age. She has been writing poems and short stories since she learned to hold a pencil.

She received her degree from the University of North Texas in Linguistics/ Technical Communication and later went on to work for several years in corporate America as a Technical Writer.

Becoming a Beautiful Articulate Person is the sequel to her debut lyrical collection, The Lyrical Journal of Sapphire Rhymes: Tear-Drop Stained Confessions. Her mission with the release of her second poetic collection is to share her story—the good, the not so good, the sad, the happy, even the raunchy moments.

No more secrets, no more lies, no more skeletons lurking in dark closets. This is her story, told her way to help someone else understand that he or she is not alone and their story makes them a Beautiful Articulate Person (B.A.P).

"I can't change the past but I can allow my past to create a better and brighter future…"

—**A. Branch**

Thank you for your purchase and your support.

Follow
me

@ABranch19

@articulatebeauty1

amber.branch.737

DO YOU HAVE A BOOK IDEA THAT YOU'VE BEEN TOILING ABOUT?

No worries. I got you! I'll coach you through the self-publishing process step by step based on my certified training from the Self-Publishing School

Contact me for an initial FREE consultation at:
amber@articulatebusinessgroup.com

THE LYRICAL JOURNAL OF SAPPHIRE RHYMES

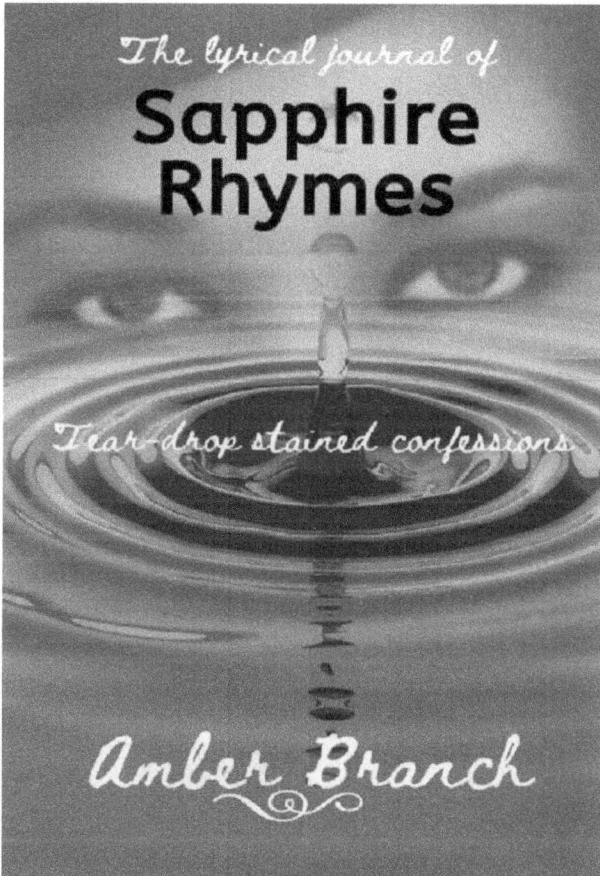

Tear-drop Stained Confessions

BECOMING A BEAUTIFUL ARTICULATE PERSON:

The Genesis of Transformation

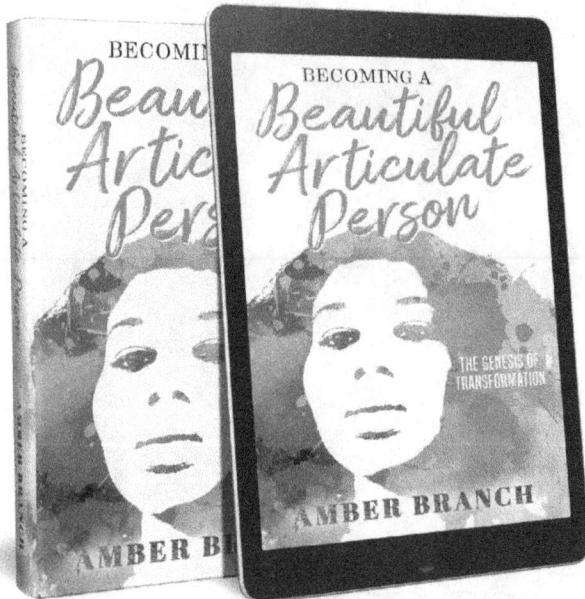

LIKE MY BOOKS?

Don't forget to leave a review!
Your review means the world to me!

Head over to Amazon or the website you purchased the book from and leave an honest review for me! Thanks a bunch! I am truly grateful!

MORE BOOKS COMING SOON...

SPOILER ALERT

To get exclusive updates on future book releases, live events & more, subscribe to my mailing list at: www.amberrbranch.com

YOUR STORY STARTS HERE?

Do not worry.
Do not stress.

Just put your thoughts on the following pages and let your heart guide you with the rest. Write down your thoughts, doodle your day-dreams or pin some inspirational quotes.

However you choose, I hope these next pages you'll use.

Become a Beautiful Articulate Person

GOT WRITER'S BLOCK?
NEED HELP GETTING STARTED?

Try this:

1. List 5 things you love about yourself and why.
2. Name 4 things that you are proud that you have accomplished.
3. Name 3 things you've overcome and what it taught you or how it changed you.
4. Name 2 people who have influenced you in your life and how?
5. Name an important event in your life and how it changed you.

Note: *After you have completed the above exercise answer the following question?* **I am changed because...**

_____

_____

_____

_____

_____

_____

_____

_____

_____

_____

_____

1ST BOOK DESCRIPTION:

Book Title: _____

Subtitle: _____

_____

Insert book cover mockup here:

Author

Your paperback should have at least one author or primary contributor.

Primary Author

_____

Contributors (Optional)

_____

_____

_____

Description

_____

_____

_____

_____

_____

HTML Description

Use this website to generate a simplified HTML –friendly description for Amazon and other websites(https://ablurb.github.io/)

_____

_____

_____

_____

Publishing Rights

Keywords

Choose up to 7 keywords that describe your book. How do I choose keywords?

Categories

2ND BOOK DESCRIPTION:

Book Title: _____

Subtitle: _____

_____

Insert book cover mockup here:

Author

Your paperback should have at least one author or primary contributor.

Primary Author

_____

Contributors (Optional)

_____

_____

_____

Description

_____

_____

_____

_____

_____

_____

HTML Description

Use this website to generate a simplified HTML –friendly description for Amazon and other websites(https://ablurb.github.io/)

_____

_____

_____

_____

Publishing Rights

_____

Keywords

Choose up to 7 keywords that describe your book. How do I choose keywords?

_____

_____

_____

_____

_____

Categories

_____

_____

_____

_____

_____

_____

_____

_____

WRITING WORKSPACE:

_____

_____

_____

_____

_____

_____

_____

_____

_____

_____

_____

_____

_____

_____

_____

_____

_____

_____

_____

BRAINSTORM PHASE:

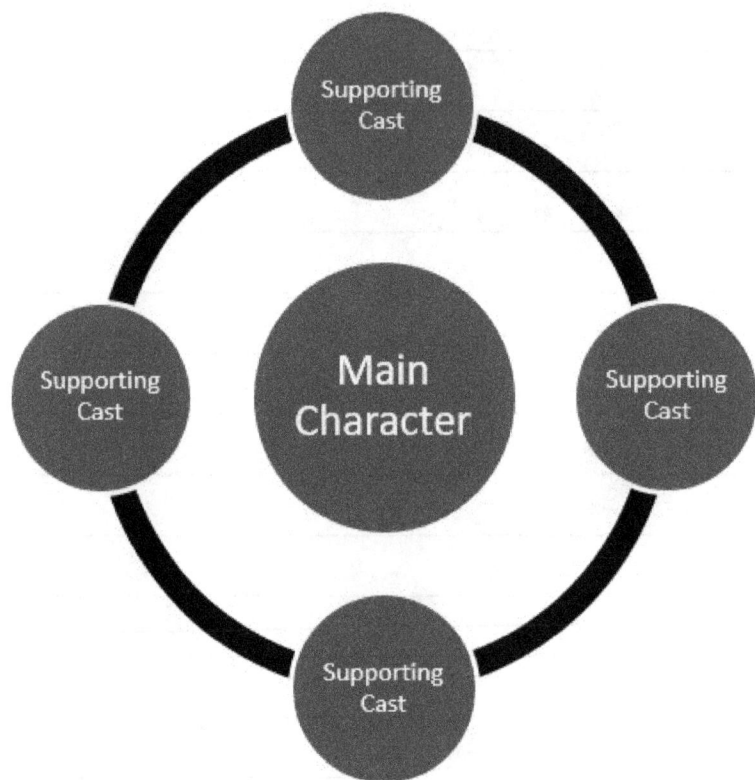

AUTHOR TO-DO LIST:

AUTHOR TO-DO LIST:

AUTHOR TO-DO LIST:

AUTHOR TO-DO LIST: